But let justice roll down like waters,
    and righteousness like an ever-flowing stream.

Amos 5:24

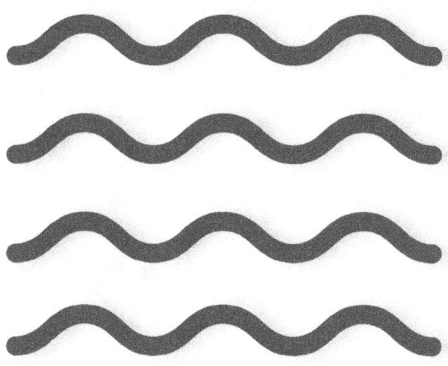

When Woke Goes Broke is a compass for Christians navigating today's wild world of political wokeism and social issues. Suzanne Choo shows us how to be bridge builders reflecting the love of Christ. It is hopeful, while tackling tough questions, reiterating God's righteous justice and love for all creation.

This book will certainly help us interpret our complex times through a biblical lens and God's metanarrative. A must-read for a genuine spiritual awakening!

Dr Goh Wei-Leong
Co-Founder, HealthServe;
Global Board, OM International & Chairman, Mercy Teams International

A clear analysis of wokeism and a helpful framework to understand it at work and how a Christian ought to approach it redemptively for a Christ-centric missional ethic. *When Woke Goes Broke* is a useful and accessible resource for Christian pastors, leaders, and practitioners of justice work which I commend heartily.

Elder Ronald J.J. Wong
National Coordinator (Micah Singapore);
Board Chairman, Bless Community Services

VOLUME 1

*When Woke Goes Broke:
Redeeming Social Justice for the Church*

Suzanne S. Choo

WHEN WOKE GOES BROKE

WHEN WOKE GOES BROKE

Redeeming Social Justice for the Church

Suzanne S. Choo

Series Editor: Leow Wen Pin

GRACEW♥RKS

**When Woke Goes Broke:
Redeeming Social Justice for the Church**

The Gospel Way Series

Copyright © 2024 Suzanne S. Choo

All rights reserved. No part of this publication may be reproduced, stored in a retrieval system, or transmitted, in any form or by any means, electronic, mechanical, photocopying, recording or otherwise, without the prior written permission of the authors, except in the case of brief quotations embodied in
critical articles and reviews.

Published by Graceworks Private Limited
22 Sin Ming Lane, #04-76 Midview City, Singapore 573969
Tel: +65 67523403
enquiries@graceworks.com.sg
www.graceworks.com.sg

All Scripture quotations, unless otherwise noted, are taken from
The Holy Bible, English Standard Version. Copyright © 2000; 2001
by Crossway Bibles, a division of Good News Publishers. Used by
permission. All rights reserved.

ISBN: 978-981-94-0083-6

Printed in Singapore

1 2 3 4 5 6 • 27 26 25 24

National Library Board, Singapore Cataloguing in Publication Data
Name(s): Choo, Suzanne S. | Leow, Wen Pin, editor.
Title: When woke goes broke : redeeming social justice for the church /
Suzanne S. Choo ; series editor, Leow Wen Pin.
Other Title(s): Gospel way series.
Description: Singapore : Graceworks Private Limited, [2024]
Identifier(s): ISBN 978-981-94-0083-6 (paperback)
Subject(s): LCSH: Social justice--Biblical teaching. | Social justice--
Religious aspects--Christianity. | Church and social problems--Asia.
Classification: DDC 261.8--dc23

*To my daughter, Gracelyn,
and the young Christians of her generation
and those to come,
may you all remain rooted in your faith
and be shining examples of God's truth and grace.*

Contents

Editor's Preface — *xiii*

CHAPTER 1 — 1
Wokeism and the Call for a Biblical Interpretation of Culture

CHAPTER 2 — 13
Political Wokeism and its Connections to Postmodernism and Post-truth

CHAPTER 3 — 33
Redeeming Social Justice: Lessons From Jonah

CHAPTER 4 — 51
Practical Approaches to Social Justice for the Church Today

Resources — *64*
Endnotes — *66*
About the Author — *71*
About the Series — *73*

Series Editor's Preface

While it might be a cliché to say that the world is rapidly changing, it is very much the lived experience of Christians in Asia! Each new year brings on fresh challenges that the Church must address, be it new technologies, social disruption, or evolving philosophies. While we know that God continues to speak today through His Word, it is not easy for Christians to apply Scripture to these new challenges in a way that is both faithful and relevant.

The Gospel Way series was formulated with this concern in mind: to address complex modern challenges through user-friendly primers that guide Christians to respond faithfully according to God's Word. This series has several distinctives. It is contextualised—written for Asians by Asians. It is thoughtfully edited, taking a biblically based approach that evangelical churches can trust. It adopts a concrete approach that helps Christians transform the way they live in a practical way. It is accessible, avoiding jargon where possible, and clearly introduces technical terms when they are needed to understand the issue at hand.

This series is also deliberately geared to supporting local churches. Each guide in the series is designed with two groups of people in mind. First, busy church leaders who need to learn quickly about emerging social issues and help their congregations respond. Second, church small groups who need robust yet practical study material to help their members grow. For this reason, discussion questions are provided at the close of each chapter to allow facilitated discussion in small-group meetings. In addition, an appendix with resources for further learning is provided at the end of each guide.

I am thankful that this inaugural volume of the series focuses on social justice which is one of the most prominent cultural trends today, especially among youth and young adults. The Church cannot afford to ignore this topic. However, perhaps because of the past excesses of liberation theology and the present problems with wokeism, churches have often shied away from meaningful engagement with social justice. This is a tragedy because, as this book will demonstrate, God Himself is deeply concerned about social justice. Churches should therefore seek to reflect God's heartbeat in their personal discipleship.

However, amidst the present cacophony of voices that advocate for or argue against wokeism, it is not easy to grasp what is a balanced and biblical view of social justice. This is why I am deeply grateful to my friend, Associate Professor Suzanne Choo, for agreeing to author this volume. She is eminently qualified to write this book. She is a world-class academic who has devoted much of her professional career to thinking and writing about the pedagogy of ethics in a changing, cosmopolitan world. She is also theologically astute. In fact, it was a thoughtful essay that she had written for an advanced Hebrew class (scoring top grades!) that first gave me the idea to invite her to pen this volume.

In this volume Suzanne helps the reader to understand wokeism—warts and all—in its historical and intellectual context. She then provides a thoughtful, biblical response to it. Her broad argument follows the title of this series—The Gospel Way—in the sense that she concludes that wokeism can be redeemed when transformed in the light of the gospel of Jesus Christ. Further, when redeemed in such a manner, she avers that a biblical approach to wokeism allows social justice to be an integral part of gospel-shaped living in the community of faith. I am grateful for her informed and even-handed treatment of the topic. Her writing style reflects the gentle yet discerning posture that she proposes that all Christians should have in order to respond wisely in an unruly world of fake news. She truly practises what she preaches.

I am thankful to our publishers, Graceworks, for believing in this series and helping to bring this inaugural volume to completion. Due to unforeseen circumstances, the logistical timeline for this volume was relatively short, but they lovingly brought this project to completion with good cheer and classic Singaporean efficiency. My warmest thanks—especially to Bernice, Priscilla, and Sarah—for their labour of love.

May this book, and The Gospel Way series, help the Church in Asia better respond to the shifting shadows of this world. Amidst all these, one thing remains true: our God is faithful and relevant!

Leow Wen Pin
Series Editor
August 2024

Wokeism and the Call for a Biblical Interpretation of Culture

On average, adults today are awake for about 16 hours each day. How do we spend these waking moments? One hundred and fifty years ago, the average adult would spend ten hours working. Today, adults spend about six hours working, thanks to technological advances that have enhanced productivity.[1] The good news is that people now have more time outside of work.

But how awake are we even in our waking moments? The philosopher Maxine Greene coined the term "wide-awakeness" out of concern that modern life was becoming more impersonal and automated. She called for a greater consciousness and a fuller attention to our social realities.[2] Like Neo in the science fiction classic movie, *The Matrix*, we can go through the motions of life, oblivious to larger powers that condition us. That is until we choose, like Neo, to become wide awake and enlightened about the invisible systems governing our lives. To be wide awake, in this sense, does not literally mean the opposite of sleeping. It means having one's eyes opened to truth, having one's senses mentally and emotionally attuned to external influences. In short, to be wide awake is to be "woke".

The term "woke" refers to being alert and attentive to injustices and discrimination. Its roots may be traced to the Civil Rights Movement in the United States. It was utilised in songs by activists protesting discrimination towards African Americans in the 1920s and 1930s.

"Woke" underwent a revival in the 2010s following a wake of incidents such as the killing of a black teenager, Trayvon Martin, by a neighbourhood watch in 2012, and the killing of Michael Brown and George Floyd, both unarmed civilians, by white police officers in 2014 and 2020, among others. These incidents sparked the Black Lives Matter movement. "Woke" became a catchword signalling the need to be conscious of implicit racism and systemic injustice. By 2017, "woke" had entered the Oxford English Dictionary and, over time, has been used as a rallying call for greater equity, freedom, and rights for marginalised groups.

In the early days, to be "woke" was regarded as being hip—it meant that one was not naive and ignorant of injustice, that one was a resistance fighter defending those who were oppressed. These days "woke" has become broke. It is a divisive term where paradoxically, the struggle for inclusivity has resulted in exclusivity and the push for diversity has led to reverse racism.

Take the case of a business professor from the University of Southern California who was discussing how Chinese speakers often use filler words such as 那个 (nà gè) in their everyday speech. The following day, a complaint letter was sent to his superiors. Black members of his class were offended by his use of 那个 which, to them, sounded like the N-word, a racial slur. The professor was asked to stop teaching the class.

However, Chinese international students felt his "cancellation" showed a disregard for communication patterns in Chinese cultures. So, while Black students cancelled the professor in the name of diversity, Chinese students found this culturally insensitive![3]

"Woke" is so much a part of culture that every other day, one reads of ordinary civilians, celebrities, and politicians being called out for discriminatory behaviour and publicly criticised. Companies increasingly engage in "woke capitalism" where corporations support socio-political movements and causes. Relatedly, buyers are demonstrating "woke consumerism" when they place social justice and ethical considerations in their purchasing decisions.

"Woke" has penetrated every aspect of culture, drawing widespread awakening to issues of justice behind what we eat and wear, the language we use, public policies, and cultural practices. Increasingly, the Church will grapple with a young generation exposed to "woke" politics and invested in social justice causes. How can the Church respond in ways that are aligned with biblical principles of justice?

Our first step is to understand that "woke" is a phenom-enon of contemporary culture and we should not be apathetic, fully receptive, or dismissive of it. Instead, if we are committed to winning others for Christ, we must first be committed to a sound biblical interpretation of culture.

THE CALL TO INTERPRET THE TIME
In Luke 12:54–56, Jesus said to the crowds:

> *When you see a cloud rising in the west, you say at once, 'A shower is coming.' And so it happens. And when you see the south wind blowing, you say, 'There will be scorching heat,' and it happens. You hypocrites! You know how to interpret the appearance of earth and sky, but why do you not know how to interpret the present time?*

Jesus' audience likely included farmers and so it was not surprising that they knew how to interpret weather patterns.[4] Yet, this was not enough if they were to be committed followers. After all, this passage follows Jesus' parables in Luke 12 that highlight the importance of being ready for the day of judgement and culminates in a revelation that His mission on earth would cause divisions, even among close family members. Jesus' central point was that we need to be both spiritually ready and discerning.

Unfortunately, human beings are prone to focus on material things that support our needs. Jesus observed that His audience had developed expertise in reading weather patterns accurately because their livelihoods depended on this. Clouds from the west suggested an impending thunderstorm; southerly winds would bring scorching heat from the desert.[5] To an agricultural community, wrong interpretations of the weather could mean an end to their livelihoods. Thus, Jesus' audience invested time and energy to perfect their ability to read the climate.

This is similar to what we often do today. While most of us are not farmers, we have likewise spent years learning to read the "material climate" of our world, such as patterns about the stock market, housing prices, and consumer trends. We too are motivated by how accurate interpretation leads to material benefits!

Jesus used a strong word to describe people absorbed in such behaviour—"hypocrites". Here, the word "hypocrite" does not refer to a liar, as we would typically infer based on our modern understanding of the term. Rather, in this context, the term refers to a counterfeit Christian. This Greek word *hypokritēs* appears two more times in the book of Luke (Luke 6:42 and 13:15). In each case, it refers to one who is self-righteous in assuming he knows the truth while focusing on what is less important. The hypocrite lacks spiritual insight while the opposite is one who has discernment. A mark of such discernment is being able to "interpret the present time" (Luke 12:56)—to discern clearly the exact social and spiritual nature of our culture.

THE IMPORTANCE OF DOUBLE INTERPRETATION

How then should Christians interpret the present time? John Stott has provided a useful strategy of "double listening" which entails listening to both God's Word and the world:

> We listen to the Word with humble reverence, anxious to understand it, and resolved to believe and obey what we have come to understand. We listen to the world with critical alertness, anxious to understand it too, and resolved not to necessarily

> believe and obey it, but to sympathise with it and to seek grace to discover how the gospel relates to it.[6]

Adapting Stott's concept, I suggest we need to adopt a double interpretation to reading the world and the Word. This means that we need to pay attention to world events and acquire the contextual knowledge and skills to interpret influential cultural phenomena, such as wokeism. More importantly, we need to deepen our understanding of God's Word so that we can interpret the world with discernment.

1. Interpreting the World by Studying Culture
To apply double interpretation, we must first interpret the world we live in. To do so, we should learn to "read" culture. The cultural identity of a group is predominantly constructed through shared language and stories about its way of life and values.[7] Thus, we can interpret culture by paying attention to language (including concepts) and stories (told through fiction, movies, music, historical narratives, and the news). We should also seek to understand patterns and movements in culture. What appears trending in social media? What

underlying philosophy and values are being promoted in contemporary movements? Who is behind this and what are their motivations? We also need to recognise that contemporary culture is a result of history. The "present time" which Jesus called us to interpret is a product of the past. So when we seek to understand contemporary culture, we need to examine not only what is occurring now, but also how the present connects to history.

Crucially, we must avoid the two extremes of either entirely conforming to or completely rejecting culture. Instead, we recognise that when Jesus, the Son of God, came to this earth, He chose to participate in human culture and yet was above culture.[8] In the same way, our authentic desire to understand culture should flow from our mission to love God and others. We transform culture by rightly seeking the restoration of God's kingdom on earth.

2. Reading the Word to Out-Narrate the World
As Romans 12:2 reminds us,

> *Do not be conformed to this world, but be*

transformed by the renewal of your mind, that by testing you may discern what is the will of God, what is good and acceptable and perfect.

Our interpretations of the world should be guided by our interpretations of the Word. This passage provides two important steps. The first begins with us. We need to be rooted in God's Word and be willing to allow scripture to confront the value systems we may have unconsciously internalised. The only safeguard against complete conformity to the world is by being transformed by God's Word. Only then can we proceed to the second step—to test, analyse, and discern the world through a biblical lens. This is fundamental to transcending cultural norms.

Looking at the world through God's Word allows us to see reality through God's eyes. We are then able to perform what Christopher Watkin, in his book *Biblical Critical Theory*, called "out-narrating"—not by "telling the better story in the sense of being the most gripping or necessarily satisfying [but] telling the bigger story, the story within which all other stories find their place."[9]

Conclusion
Wokeism is gaining momentum around the world and this calls for church leaders to empower their congregations to engage in double interpretation—interpreting the world through the Word.

In this book, our focus is on political wokeism, a form of social justice arising from our hyper-globalised, digitally connected, twenty-first century. How can we interpret today's wokeism through the lens of Scripture? The aim is to return to an understanding of social justice in the light of the gospel.

We begin, in Chapter 2, by exploring the historical influences of political wokeism, particularly its relationship with two other movements—postmodernism and post-truth. In Chapter 3, we consider how Christians can provide a different perspective to secular wokeism. We do so by turning to God's Word—specifically, the book of Jonah—to provide a Christian approach to social justice. Finally, in Chapter 4, we discuss practical approaches to social justice that churches can apply.

≈ REFLECTION QUESTIONS

1. Read Luke 12:49–59. What did Jesus say about His purpose on earth? How does this relate to His call to interpret the present time?

2. Pick a television series, movie, computer game, or song that has been influential or popular in your community or country in the last five years. What underlying message and values are being proposed?

3. What concepts or ideas are trending on social media today? What insights do they provide about secular worldviews today? To what extent do they align with Christian values? How would you interpret the world through God's Word? Provide examples from Scripture.

Political Wokeism and its Connections to Postmodernism and Post-truth

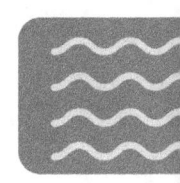

Wokeism is on the rise today, particularly among youths around the world. From climate change to gun control, bullying, and access to clean water, among others, youths are calling on governments to take action on social and global issues. In a report on youth civic engagement, the United Nations observes that worldwide, youths today are "much more concerned than previous generations with human rights and environmental causes."[1]

In Singapore, a survey of youths by the National Youth Council reports that civic participation has risen among youths. Close to nine in ten youths participate in at least one form of civic activity and the percentage of youth participation has risen from 65 percent in 2016 to 88 percent in 2019.[2]

Compared to previous generations, youths are more "woke" to injustices. What has also changed is the politicised nature of wokeism. While wokeism originally referred to a general state of being alert to injustice, it has increasingly been used as a tool to advance ideological agendas especially since the 2010s. Liberals and progressives have called their followers to be "woke" in order to garner support for political campaigns and movements.

There are three dominant aspects of activism involving the fight (i) against racism by Black Lives Matter activists; (ii) against sexism and sexual harassment by activists of the #metoo movement; and (iii) for gender inclusivity by the LGBTQIA+ community. Thus, it is more accurate to describe twenty-first-century "woke" culture as political wokeism.

Political wokeism has contributed to a renewed sensitivity towards interpretation, especially the ways people interpret culture and identity. The following are some examples of concepts derived from "woke" interpretations of culture:

- **BoPo**—This refers to body positivity. BoPo is a social movement that is involved in disrupting cultural interpretations of the body that promote a social ideal and replacing this with alternative interpretations that celebrate the body in all forms.
- **Conscious capitalism**—This refers to being consciously aware of the impact of capitalist profit-making so that businesses can incorporate greater social responsibility and create value for all stakeholders (customers, employees, investors, society, the environment).
- **Cultural appropriation**—This refers to the adoption or exploitation of another culture (such as food, music, clothing) for one's purposes, often for entertainment, without showing proper respect or understanding of that culture.
- **Gender fluidity and gender performativity**—This refers to un-fixing gender binaries and re-interpreting how a person can express or interpret gender (feminine, masculine, neutral, androgynous, etc.) across a spectrum, in combination, and in shifting ways.[3]

- **Identity privilege**—This refers to being conscious of the invisible privileges tied to one's own class, race, gender, etc., so that success is not assumed to be based on one's own effort alone. For example, social justice scholars have explored how white privilege has historically contributed to racism through built-in advantages leading to greater access to power and resources.
- **Intersectionality**—This has been used to support the idea that interpretations of injustice should account for multidimensional and intersecting domains of discrimination. Kimberlé Crenshaw, who is credited with coining the term, gives the example of a traffic intersection to highlight the fact that a person may experience double, triple, multiple layers of oppression including racism, colonialism, patriarchy, etc.[4]

As a movement, political wokeism has benefits and weaknesses. It is beneficial in surfacing implicit biases that may be deeply embedded in culture. For example, the practice of brownface in which lighter-skinned people portray themselves as dark-skinned, often for entertainment, may not have generated controversy before. However, in recent years, "woke" culture has foregrounded how such actions reinforce stereotypes and the subjugation of minorities.

Political wokeism has also been criticised for perpetuating a hyper-sensitivity to power where every issue is interpreted in terms of violence and oppression. One consequence is that people may become obsessed with political correctness. One recent phenomenon involves explicitly indicating gender pronouns next to one's name in email signatures, such as "Jane Doe (she/her/hers, he/him/his, or they/them/theirs)". The idea is that people should have the agency to name their gender identity and others should not impose their assumptions. However, this raises the question: Would a person be seen as non-inclusive if this person did not indicate his/her pronoun? Also, why should gender be the dominant identity indicator of a person? Can a Jane Doe identify as Christian/mother/teacher?

One key problem with political correctness is its associations with "call out" and "cancel" culture. When one does not conform to expected behaviour, a common tactic by "woke" groups is to publicly criticise and

shame the offender, leading others to ostracise him/
her. The pervasive use of social media now allows
everyone to become a digital activist. For the Church
to respond rightly, we need to "interpret the present
time", i.e., to discern culture in context.

So, how did wokeism become the political wokeism
we see today? I argue that political wokeism cannot
be understood apart from two other cultural trends—
postmodernism and post-truth. Taken together, these
3Ps (political wokeism, postmodernism, and post-truth)
constitute the dominant cultural ethos of our time. In
what follows, I provide an overview of postmodernism
and post-truth before explaining how they have influenced the form of political wokeism we have today.

POSTMODERNISM

One significant attribute of political wokeism is the loss
of faith in authority, coupled with increased scepticism
that political systems have become unjust by securing
the power of elites. Where did this way of thinking stem
from? About three centuries ago during the Enlighten-
ment, Western culture was more hopeful. Key scientific
breakthroughs were made, such as Newton's gravity

and Copernican theory, along with revolutionary theories such as Darwin's theory of evolution and Freud's psychoanalysis. The scientific revolution cemented mankind's faith in scientific rationality and progress.

However, faith in scientific and technological progress was severely disrupted by two major world wars. Postmodernism emerged following the end of the Second World War. The notion of "post-" implies both a continuation as well as a break with modernism. On one hand, postmodernism continued and even intensified modernism's emphasis on individualism. For example, events such as the Holocaust provided greater recognition of the need for individual autonomy given the large-scale oppression of entire communities. On the other hand, postmodernism provided a stronger sense of disillusionment towards authority and truth claims.

The quintessential quote that encapsulates the spirit of postmodernism is from the French philosopher Jean-Francois Lyotard—"Simplifying to the extreme, I define postmodern as incredulity toward metanarratives."[5] This refers to a scepticism towards all truth claims such as science, truth, progress, and religion.

In short, postmodernism has been described as an antifoundational philosophy.[6]

Aside from the horrors of totalitarianism exemplified in the world wars, another reason for the growing scepticism towards truth was the intensification of globalisation. Advances in technology, particularly in communication, meant that countries were connected more closely than in any other period in human history. This created conditions for hyper-capitalism in which global exchanges of goods, services, and information have intensified in terms of speed and across distances, leading to the penetration of commercial interests in every aspect of human life.

As a result, Lyotard argued that even scientific claims to truth can no longer be objective.[7] Such distrust of scientific facts extended to a distrust of reality. Another Postmodern philosopher, Jean Baudrillard, observed that our reliance on technology has caused us to live in a world of simulations in which the virtual feels more real than reality itself.[8] The result is that people are led to trust an illusion presented by the media (and those who control it) rather than to pursue the truth of reality itself.

If postmodernism perpetuated a scepticism towards truth, it was not surprising that this scepticism extended towards all forms of authority. A key strategy that many cultural critics adopt is poststructuralism, a method for critiquing truth claims as well as social structures.

Poststructuralism (and its associated branches of Marxism, feminism, postcolonialism) is concerned with the ways dominant groups use language and interpretation to obtain and maintain power. Prominent philosophers such as Jacques Derrida and Michel Foucault influenced poststructuralist scholars to identify gaps, contradictions, and ideological agendas behind dominant concepts, authoritative historical accounts, and systems of power.

In short, poststructuralism supports a way of interpreting culture (known as a "hermeneutics of suspicion") where readers are encouraged to be more critical and read more deeply into underlying structures of thought. On one hand, this is beneficial in sensitising readers to subtexts, biases, and value systems inherent in all media. In this sense, poststructuralism pushes us to not naively accept what a text or its author communicates at face value. On the other hand, poststructuralism, taken to the extreme, can lead to unending scepticism towards any kind of argument, including an argument for God, ultimately leading to nihilism.

POST-TRUTH

As we head into the third decade of the twenty-first century, postmodernism has morphed further into post-truth. This essentially normalises postmodernism's attitude of scepticism to the point that it becomes typical to accept that there can be many alternative truths.

In 2016, Oxford dictionaries declared "post-truth" as its word of the year observing that it is becoming a mainstay in political commentary. Post-truth is defined as "relating to or denoting circumstances in which objective facts are less influential in shaping public opinion than appeals to emotion and personal belief."[9] The term became popularised by key political events such as Brexit and Donald Trump's presidential nomination. Other contributing factors include the prevalence of sock puppets (fake online accounts) and deep fake technologies. The popularity of social media platforms has also allowed individuals to spread and create disinformation. The rise of post-truth has contributed to two effects.

The first effect is that, because all truth claims can no longer be believed, the individual becomes the one who decides what is true. For example, the well-known Polish sociologist, Zygmunt Bauman, argued that postmodernism is "morality without [an] ethical code."[10] In other words, we can no longer depend upon a universally agreed set of codes. Instead, he proposed that morality must be re-personalised, which means moral responsibility lies with the individual, giving the sense that one has power to choose the values one wishes to abide by.

The pervasive use of social media perpetuates the crafting of individual narratives. Individuals "perform" their identities through a myriad of choices they make, such as what they will wear or how they will pose for a publicly uploaded image or video. The individual is presumed the autonomous storyteller as he/she constructs a narrative of the self. In her book, *Christian Ethics for a Digital Society*, Katherine Ott observes,

> Social media creates a space where humans become *produsers* (producer + user) and *prosumers* (producer + consumer) of technology and information more generally.[11] (italics added)

Consequently, technology facilitates the stories we tell about ourselves and, in this sense, we become "digitally embodied" when the online identities we construct become an appendage of who we are. The digital self is encapsulated in "I share and therefore I am".[12]

To be clear, I am not suggesting that technology and social media should be rejected. They have many benefits, including providing powerful opportunities to participate actively in social justice issues. What Christians should take heed of is the danger when postmodernism and post-truth become engines driving political "woke" culture.

THE 3PS IN COMBINATION: POLITICAL WOKEISM, POSTMODERNISM, AND POST-TRUTH

The form of wokeism that has taken shape today integrates the deadly 3Ps (political wokeism, postmodernism, post-truth). This creates a lethal combination that potentially contributes to greater polarisation and anarchy in societies today. In particular, three dangers may emerge.

1. Political Wokeism + Postmodernism = Social Justice Without Accountability

The first danger is when individuals are attentive to social justice but are driven by postmodern scepticism. They can turn into online "vigilantes", out to exert their own self-righteous morality through cancel culture, characterised by belligerent language and aggressive behaviour.

A study by researchers from Yale University highlighted how social media platforms amplify expressions of outrage. Users learn, over time, that stronger and more extreme language is rewarded with increasing "likes" and "shares". Gradually, moderate users become less moderate.[13] Further, on social media, cancelling others is made easier since individuals can hide their true identities behind their virtual usernames or avatars. Yet, for Christians, social justice should not occur outside of accountability to God or the Church. As we will explore in the next chapter, when God calls out injustice, it is not meant to cancel individuals, but to redeem and restore them to Himself.

2. Political Wokeism + Post-truth = Social Justice Without Informed Justice

The second danger is when "woke" individuals are themselves purveyors of post-truths. Social media messages are often quickly forwarded to others without ascertaining their accuracy or credibility. When individuals think they are the judges of truth and morality, there is a disregard for other perspectives that may be equally valid.

Another study by Yale University researchers found that, when faced with a flood of information, individuals will filter what they read to reinforce their own existing beliefs.[14] Algorithms on social media are programmed to present information based on what the individual already subscribes to. Otherwise known as "confirmation bias", individuals may then solidify their beliefs and become less open to different perspectives. For example, many called the Dalai Lama "sick" and a "paedophile" in a viral video of him apparently asking a boy to "suck his tongue". It was later revealed that his words were mistranslated. Tibetans explained that sticking out the tongue is a traditional sign of respect in their culture.[15] Thus, when individuals advocate for social justice without being fully informed of the facts, what occurs is the opposite of justice!

3. Political Wokeism + Postmodernism + Post-truth = Idolatry of the Self

Finally, the threefold combination of political wokeism, postmodernism, and post-truth reinforces self-idolatry. A fashionable concept in postmodern thought is "performativity". Popularised by the feminist, poststructuralist philosopher Judith Butler, performativity denotes how an individual's identity is performed through repetitive acts so that these acts constitute who we are.[16]

Performativity has been used to support the postmodern view of individual autonomy where an individual can choose to narrate his/her identity (gender, race, class, etc.) in fluid rather than fixed ways, taking on a mixture of identities from one moment to the next.

Added to this, the climate of post-truth supports the idolatry of the individual where truth-seeking is no longer a priority. Instead, it is replaced by truth-selection—we select the "truth" that best fits the identity we create. This perpetuates an over-individualistic form of wokeism. Under the banner of the fight to alleviate injustice for others, our primary concern ironically becomes the elevation of our own rights, entitlements, and beliefs—often at the expense of other voices and perspectives.

Today's postmodern-post-truth form of political wokeism conditions one to view identity as culturally determined either by one's society or one's choices. Yet, for Christians, if our identity is in Christ, then our identity must transcend cultural determinism. We are part of God's divine plan and God is actively shaping our identities beyond the politics and trends of culture.

Further, while postmodern performativity has been used to push for individual reclamation of identity, our God-given identities as Christians serve a larger purpose—to reflect Christ. As Galatians 2:20 reminds us:

> *I have been crucified with Christ. It is no longer I who live, but Christ who lives in me. And the life I*

now live in the flesh I live by faith in the Son of God, who loved me and gave himself for me.

CONCLUSION

Let me summarise this chapter: we have explored the 3Ps that characterise the "present time"—political wokeism, postmodernism, and post-truth. For the Church, each aspect has its own opportunity for advancing God's kingdom on earth. For example, postmodern practices such as poststructuralism can be used to develop discernment regarding underlying ideologies in culture; post-truth can challenge parochial and narrow worldviews, giving space to marginalised voices; and political wokeism can empower people to be actively engaged in issues of social justice for the poor and oppressed.

However, I have highlighted how each aspect has its risks—an anti-foundational worldview, the elevation of individualised truth and morality, and the lack of accountability. In combination, the 3Ps perpetuate the sense that we can become our own god of morality and spirituality. What then are some biblical principles Christians can adopt to "out-narrate" and tell the bigger story that would draw others to God? This is the focus of the next chapter.

≋ REFLECTION QUESTIONS

1. Reflect on some of the comments and reactions you have given through chat tools or social media. What motivates your posts or reactions? How would you describe your online or virtual behaviour and how does this align with your own values?

2. What are your thoughts on the 3Ps (political wokeism, postmodernism, and post-truth)? Give examples of how you have observed each of these or combinations of these in recent days. What biblical principles can we apply to guide our response?

3. Read Ephesians 5:1–2, 11–17. What does it mean to walk in love? How might this inform the ways we speak and behave in public spaces, particularly in the ways we relate to others both in person and virtually?

Redeeming Social Justice: Lessons From Jonah

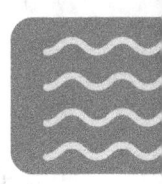

Social justice may be a fashionable term today associated with influential celebrities and activists. What is less known is that the term originated in the early nineteenth century. The Italian Jesuit priest, Luigi Taparelli (1793–1862), reportedly first employed the term "social justice" in response to unjust economic and social conditions of his time.[1]

The predominant response of the Catholic Church to poverty then was to call for an expansion of charitable works. Taparelli argued that this was insufficient. Rather than a top-down reliance on authorities (such as the government or the Church) and rather than passive acts of charity, Taparelli argued for active civic participation from the ground up. Societies, in his view, would become more just when citizens find solidarity within communities and work in unity to promote just conditions for others.[2]

For Taparelli, social justice was deemed a virtue premised on the individual's disposition to protect and support others. This was a more communitarian and duty-bound vision of social justice compared to politically "woke" social justice today characterised by an aggressive activism aimed at advancing the agenda of an individual or group.

How can Christians conceptualise a different perspective to today's political wokeism? In this chapter, I explore a theory of social justice from a Christian perspective through studying the book of Jonah. In this manner, I intend to do what was described in Chapter 1—to read the world through God's Word and so to "interpret the present time" through biblical lenses.

SOCIAL JUSTICE IN THE BOOK OF JONAH

Right at the beginning, God's Word is given to Jonah in the form of a commission:[3] "Arise, go to Nineveh, that great city, and call out against it, for their evil has come up before me" (Jonah 1:2). The Hebrew word for "arise" (*qum*) is typically used to describe the action of rising up, to make a move.[4] This suggests that Jonah was in a state of passivity, while God is the initiator who tells him to arise to act, and, in modern terms, to "stay woke to injustice".

The call to arise is followed by two verbs that convey both physical movement (to "go to Nineveh") and metaphorical awakening to injustice (to "call out against it"). The act of "calling out" refers to making a proclamation against the Ninevites for their injustices. So we see that the call to be "woke" and to call out injustice are not modern-day phenomena but found at the beginning of the book of Jonah! In what follows, I highlight three key ideas from Jonah that may help us understand what it means to be "woke" from a Christian perspective.

1. SPIRITUAL WOKENESS BEFORE POLITICAL WOKENESS

One essential attribute of God is His concern with justice. Throughout the Bible, God calls His people to be spiritually "woke" from corruption. In Jonah, this becomes evident when we consider how the subject of evil is introduced. The book begins with God explaining why He wants Jonah to go to Nineveh and issue a prophetic calling out—because "their evil has come up before me" (Jonah 1:2). God's justice is a response to man's evil ways and is to be distinguished from two secular forms of justice demonstrated in the book.

The two most common secular frameworks of justice are consequentialism and deontology. Let's consider consequentialism first. If justice is premised on the fundamental question "what is the right thing to do?",[5] then consequentialists argue that the right thing to do is one that would yield the best outcome.

One popular version of consequentialism is utilitarianism—maximising the greatest happiness for the greatest number. We can see how utilitarianism is applied in what immediately follows God's commission to Jonah.

Jonah flees and finds a ship going to Tarshish and God sends a mighty tempest. The mariners who are worshippers of other gods (Jonah 1:5) recognise that evil has come upon them (Jonah 1:7) and their approach to justice is to sacrifice one to save the majority. In this case, the lot falls on Jonah and, despite their own internal struggle to throw him overboard, Jonah himself persuades them to do so as the sea becomes more tempestuous. What we observe here is a utilitarian logic to justice. To the Gentile mariners, justice (expressed in the act of throwing Jonah overboard) is necessary to avert evil and preserve their lives.

At the same time, we observe another form of secular justice at play. Deontologists, unlike consequentialists, subscribe to the view that justice, as the right thing to do, should not be determined by good outcomes but by moral principles. One should not resort to a cost-benefit analysis when calculating what would yield best outcomes because doing so may disregard the welfare of minorities.

Instead, right action should be based on fundamental universal principles. The philosopher Immanuel Kant proposed that such a principle, governed by reason, is the imperative to treat others as an end and never as a means.[6] A version of this principle is found in the emphasis on the inherent dignity of all human beings, a core tenet of the Universal Declaration of Human Rights. Universal codes function to remind us that individuals and governments are accountable to moral standards of conduct that transcend self and nation-centric goals.

Returning to Jonah, we can see how our prophet applies deontology in his resistance to God's commission. Jonah disagrees with God's justice to the Ninevites. This comes across strongly when the same verb "to rise" (*qum*) issued in God's initial commission in Jonah 1:2 is repeated but juxtaposed with the next verb "to flee" (*barach*) in Jonah 1:3. Jonah rises to flee rather than to obey. Since Tarshish lies in the opposite direction of Nineveh,[7] Jonah's escape to Tarshish symbolises his complete disagreement with God's plan.

There are at least two reasons for this. First, throughout the book, two adjectives are most commonly ascribed to Nineveh—that it is a great city (1:2; 3:2, 4:11) and it is associated with evil (1:2; 3:8; 3:10). This combination suggests it is a city of great power, wielding violence and cruelty with few repercussions. Even the king of Nineveh, in calling for repentance, tells his people, "Let everyone turn from his evil way and from the violence that is in his hands" (Jonah 3:8), suggesting that violence was already normalised as part of their culture. Nineveh is mentioned in Genesis 10:11, leading scholars to suggest that it was closely associated with the emergence of Assyria as a nation and served to represent Assyrian imperialist expansion as well as its reputation for unrestrained cruelty and savage power.[8] The idiomatic phrase "for their evil has come up before me" (Jonah 1:2) emphasises the culmination of their evil—it was so profound that divine intervention was needed.[9]

Second, Jonah, along with the original audience, would recognise that prophetic messages were not irrevocable statements of fact but served as advance warning.[10] In other words, the proclamation was not meant to destroy transgressors but to open the possibility for their repentance.

It is this very thought that angers Jonah, so much so that he prefers death to living (Jonah 4:3), where death is the ultimate act of resistance as it would remove him from God's redemptive plan. To Jonah, God is simply not just. From a historical-critical perspective, scholars have suggested that the authors and intended audience knew that even though Nineveh was destroyed later, it had come close to destroying Israel.[11] If just principles are meant to protect the welfare of all human beings, then why would God allow an oppressive group like the Ninevites to repent only for them to continue their evil ways later on, to oppress the Israelites, and be destroyed themselves later, as described in the book of Nahum?

Jonah's view of justice is deontological, where justice should be established on moral principles consistently applied. By allowing a wicked city to go unpunished, God not only appears unfair, He is also inconsistent (given that Israel had previously been punished for idolatry).

However, God demonstrates a version of justice that transcends secular forms, particularly consequentialism and deontology. God's justice is foremost concerned with the spiritual condition of people rather than outcomes or bestowing judgements. Throughout the Old Testament, justice and righteousness together form a hendiadys—a literary expression in which a single complex idea is created by two connected words[12] (other examples are found in 1 Kings 10:9; Jer. 33:15;

Amos 5:24; Ps. 97:2; Prov. 21:3).

This complex idea of justice as righteousness explains God's response to the Ninevites' evil ways. God is concerned not merely with their outward behaviour, but with their internal disposition—that the people "do not know their right hand from their left" (Jonah 4:11). This idiomatic phrase exemplifies the pervasiveness of corruption that has so infected the entire state and heart of a person. It is similarly employed in other passages to convey a warning against idolatry (Deut. 28:14, Josh. 1:7; 23:6) or to highlight a travesty against what is morally right in the eyes of God (2 Kings 22:2, Prov. 4:27).

If righteousness is a fundamental quality of God's justice, another concept is also closely associated with justice—love. For example, in Deuteronomy 10:18, we are told that God "executes justice for the fatherless and the widow, and loves the sojourner, giving him food and clothing" (see also Ps. 33:5; 89:14; 101:1). God's justice marries both righteousness and love. Jonah understands the very heart of God's justice—that it does not consist of righteous judgements in isolation but is ultimately driven by love: "For I knew that you are a gracious God and merciful, slow to anger and abounding in steadfast love, and relenting from disaster" (Jonah 4:2). So, while the beginning of the book sets up God's justice as righteous judgement, it is the last verse that uncovers the driving force behind this—"and should not I pity Nineveh" (Jonah 4:11). God's righteousness demands judgement but His love drives the call for repentance.

This justice-righteousness-love sequence is repeated throughout the Old Testament, such as during the fall of Adam and Eve, the flood, the golden calf, etc. Time and again, a cycle is repeated. Man repents only to sin again as the Ninevites demonstrate.

Thankfully, God's justice is "abounding in steadfast love" (*hesed*) (Jonah 4:2), defined in various lexicons as "abundant kindness" or "abounding in faithfulness".[13] In other verses (e.g., Exod. 34:6, Num. 14:18, Joel 2:13), *hesed* highlights God's characteristic traits of mercy, grace, and unwavering love for mankind. The steadfast love of God endures despite man's propensity to sin.

God's justice as righteousness and love implies that the kind of Christian wokeness we are called to is, first of all, a spiritual rather than political wokeness. Spiritual wokeness is not an abstract feeling; it entails an awakening to our own spiritual state and condition before God. It involves a realisation of how sin has pervaded our souls and infected our behaviour.

When the people of Nineveh received Jonah's prophecy, they were convicted and subsequently they repented. This led the king to call for a change in their behaviour which also meant a call to change their cultural practices (Jonah 3:8).

2. CALLING OUT INJUSTICE LEADS TO CALLING TO GOD AND CALLING IN THE SINNER

Unlike secular wokeism, the book of Jonah illustrates how the calling out of injustice is not meant to cancel another group. Social media is rife with examples of vigilante justice at work where individuals often employ aggressive language to name and shame. As we have pointed out, the ultimate goal of cancellation is sadly to elevate oneself and one's own point of view at the expense of another. Conversely in Jonah, we see how calling out is antithetical to the cancelling of people. When Jonah finally obeys and goes to Nineveh to call out (*qara*) God's judgement (Jonah 3:4), the people repent and the king instructs them to call out (*qara*) mightily with all their hearts to God (Jonah 3:8). Here, we see how spiritual justice involves a calling out of sin leading to a calling to God and a calling in of the sinner. In short, redeeming others for God is the primary goal of what it means to be "woke" from a Christian perspective.

Essentially, God's justice is concerned with the redemption of man's character and spiritual state. Justice that prioritises spiritual redemption differs from consequential justice that focuses on good outcomes (such as the preservation of another group) or deontological justice that focuses on consistently applying moral codes (such as the law) or universal principles. This does not mean that God does not apply consequentialist or deontological justice but that His justice also transcends these.

This book highlights problems with consequentialist and deontological justice. Consequentialist justice leads the Gentile mariners to be concerned with the preservation of their own lives while disregarding the safety of the outsider, Jonah. Deontological justice leads to technical judgements of expected codes of behaviour that disregard the place of mercy and grace. If anything, God's justice as righteousness and love provides a powerful image of God who is not calculating (as consequentialist justice would demand) or cold (as deontological justice would demand) but who is invested in redeeming fallen humanity.

The question at the ending of Jonah shows that God remains troubled by man's continued moral depravity, but this cliff-hanger anticipates Christ, the one who is "greater than Jonah" (Matt. 12:41). Christ's intertextual reference to Jonah allows us to contrast Jonah, the imperfect mediator of man, against Christ, the perfect one. While Jonah resists God's call, Christ willingly obeys; while Jonah refuses to preach to the Gentiles, Christ reaches out to both Jews and Gentiles; while Jonah dwells on his own comfort, Christ sacrifices Himself even for a society who hated Him.

Thus, Christ represents our exemplary model of one who is the "light of the world" (John 8:12) and who calls His people to walk as children of light (Eph. 5:8). Wokeism redeemed by the gospel is rooted in love for God and for mankind. Our selfish self is turned towards God and the Other, reflecting the very character of Christ.

3. THE CHURCH AS AMBASSADORS OF GOD'S JUSTICE, RIGHTEOUSNESS AND LOVE

God could have used any means to proclaim the message of impending doom to the Ninevites in a bid to get them to repent. However, the book of Jonah shows God's commitment to work with His people as ambassadors of His justice. In effect, God's justice as righteousness and love opens the space for a relational approach to justice rather than cold, calculating executions that would have been applied through consequentialist and deontological forms of justice. As part of the genre of prophetic books, Jonah is distinct because it is structured as a pedagogical book whose emphasis is on teaching Jonah—and the audience— God's perspective on justice.[14]

The pedagogical emphasis comes across clearly in the final chapter when God patiently conveys an object lesson to help Jonah re-orientate his priorities. A plant grows to provide Jonah shade but later dies. Jonah pities the plant but is, in actual fact, pitying himself—his focus is on how the plant has failed to provide him shade against the scorching heat![15] This incident serves to highlight how God's pity for the Ninevites is different because it is not self-seeking, but outwardly focused on the spiritual wellbeing of the people.

Jonah's anger towards the plant reveals his own hypocrisy because he had put no effort in growing the plant and yet expected God's provision. What right did he have in not wanting God to similarly extend grace to the Ninevites? Similarly, Jonah had ironically praised God for saving him earlier despite his rebellion (Jonah 2:9) but he cannot accept God's mercy bestowed on others.

The pedagogical lesson highlights how God does not merely use His people as vessels for His message. He is also interested in their growth and in cultivating a relationship with them. Despite the various trials that Jonah undergoes, perhaps what is most moving is not only the authentic and open conversations he has with

God, it is also that God remains with Jonah throughout (when Jonah flees, and when he enters and leaves Nineveh). In every chapter, God's presence remains with Jonah, exemplifying His steadfast love that pursues even the one who rebels, questions, and protests. What a privilege when God calls us as His messengers. He patiently nurtures us even in our stubbornness and, in the process, we gain a greater understanding of God's heart and learn to see as He sees.

While Jonah may have felt alone in the mission, Christ, the greater Jonah, initiates a new approach to justice through the community of the Church. Jesus walked with His disciples who, in turn, along with others, established the Church.

A core purpose of the Church is to reveal God to the world, counter to spiritual and worldly ideologies as Paul states in Ephesians 3:10: "through the church the manifold wisdom of God might now be made known to the rulers and authorities in the heavenly places." This revelation of God occurs via the Church not only in the teaching of the Word but in the living out of the gospel including its practices of justice, righteousness, and love.

CONCLUSION

In summary, justice is central to God's character and what He calls us to do. However, it is distinct from secular social justice in its purposes, tone, and form. Its purpose is primarily aimed at redeeming and reconciling man to God. Its tone integrates a concern for justice and righteousness via a spirit of love and sacrifice for another. Its form is expressed in concrete practices through the Church. In the next chapter, we will explore some of the concrete ways that the Church can be a beacon of justice through its work with the poor and marginalised.

≋ REFLECTION QUESTIONS

1. Read the book of Jonah. In what ways are the lessons we learn from this book relevant to today's politically "woke", postmodern, and post-truth culture?

2. Think of specific examples of injustice you have witnessed or experienced. How would you apply the principle of calling out injustice that leads to calling to God and calling in of the sinner in these instances?

3. How did Jesus respond to the social justice issues of His time? Some examples are the issue of the woman in adultery (John 8:1–11); healing on the Sabbath (Matt. 12:9–14); paying taxes to Caesar (Mark 12:13–17); etc. What biblical principles can we draw from these in applying a Christian approach to social justice?

Practical Approaches to Social Justice for the Church Today

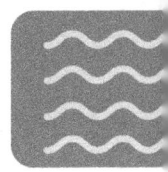

What does right action look like in today's climate of political wokeism as influenced by the principles of postmodernism and post-truth? One popular trend is clicktivism, which refers to digital activism occurring through online commenting, liking or sharing posts, signing online petitions, using social change hashtags that support a particular cause, etc.

Yet, if Christians are to be the salt and light of the world (Matt. 5:13–14), we need to practise the kind of justice characteristic of God. In what follows, I offer three practical principles the Church can apply.

1. ROOTING OURSELVES IN THE TRUTH OF GOD'S WORD
Christian wokeness emerges from being rooted in the truth of God's Word. God's truth should be the primary

driver behind the ways we interpret and respond to culture. This is because truth is a central quality of God and Christians should likewise reflect a truth-seeking disposition. Truth is the very essence of the Father— Jesus says of God "your word is truth" (John 17:17).

Likewise, Jesus embodies grace and truth, declaring, "I am the way, and the truth, and the life" (John 14:6). Truth also reflects the character of the Holy Spirit, who is described as "the Spirit of truth" (John 15:26). Unlike postmodern subscriptions to a plurality of truths, truth in these verses is in the singular. Truth is determined by God rather than culturally determined. It is objective in the sense that God has revealed Himself to creation and this revelation is not dependent on subjective feelings, desires, or beliefs of created beings.[1]

For the Church, this means we must remain committed to truth despite contemporary cultural trends that increasingly disparage, mock, and even persecute any person who subscribes to any certainty of truth. This means investing time in studying Scripture and growing deep in the Word of God. Colossians 2:6–8 supports such a conviction:

Therefore, as you received Christ Jesus the Lord, so walk in him, rooted and built up in him and established in the faith, just as you were taught, abounding in thanksgiving. See to it that no one takes you captive by philosophy and empty deceit, according to human tradition, *according to the elemental spirits of the world, and not according to Christ.* (emphasis added)

This passage provides an important theological scaffold. First, having received Christ, one must continue to strengthen one's rootedness in the faith. The second part of the passage shifts to a warning that the philosophies of the world are captivating but ultimately empty and deceitful.

Postmodernism is an example of a "cool" philosophy in its apparent openness to a plurality of views and a commitment to nothing. But postmodernism ultimately leads to spiritual shallowness and death. Thus, in the second stage, when one is rooted to God's Word, one stands on solid ground and becomes less easily taken in and shaken by the trends of the world.

2. ALLOWING RIGHT INTERPRETATION TO PRECEDE RIGHT ACTION

In a world of instantaneous information, right action (or what people believe is right) often precedes right interpretation. However, Christians need to guard against reactivism. We should pursue right interpretation before we act or react.

Right interpretation involves the fundamental disposition of truth-seeking. At a basic level, this means that we should make it a habit to apply critical literacy in our daily responses to the information we receive lest we become purveyors of post-truth ourselves. The following are some practical approaches:

- **Check data sources**—Where is the information from? Is it from a credible source, e.g., linked to a university or reputable media company? What methodologies did they use to derive their findings or arguments?
- **Triangulate data**—Compare the information across multiple sources, especially established sources. This is especially important if the information is from an unknown, newer, or less familiar organisation.

- **Seek authentic information**—If the information is not from a primary source, it is important to either verify with the primary source or, if this is not possible, understand the culture concerned so that the information can be contextualised. It is important not to impose our own cultural worldviews on those from a different culture in an uninformed fashion.
- **Listen to a different perspective**—Instead of only listening to one side of the story, it is important to understand the viewpoints of those on the other side. Empathise before you analyse.

At a more advanced level, we can apply poststructuralist interpretive strategies to analyse the information given. Although I have previously argued in Chapter 2 that poststructuralism supports postmodern scepticism towards authority, we should not simply throw the baby out with the bath water.

Poststructuralism can be useful in helping us critically read the value systems and assumptions underlying cultural trends. When interpreting a "woke" issue in our culture, we can apply the following poststructuralist questions:

- **Representation**—Who is represented in the issue concerned? Whose voice is dominant and which race, class, gender or other group does he/she represent? Whose voice is absent?
- **Bias and Stereotypes**—What are the assumptions, biases, and stereotypes underlying the arguments?
- **Privilege**—Who benefits from the effects of the arguments? Who may be disadvantaged?
- **Contextual Influence**—What social, political, economic, and historical influences have contributed to this present phenomenon?
- **Values and Worldviews**—What are the underlying values, beliefs, and worldviews that are being promoted through this text?

Poststructuralism can be helpful in pushing us to look beyond pop culture's entertainment value to discern the values underlying the books, movies, music, and other media we engage with. We also need to critically read the world through God's Word so that our evaluations of culture are biblically informed.

Third, there is also a need for pastors and church leaders to deepen hermeneutical literacy in their congregation. With the spread of disinformation, there is a greater need to sharpen the interpretive capacities of church members. One way is by incorporating interpretive skills rather than mere content in church teaching. Such teaching would go beyond the provision of knowledge to helping church members apply the skills of interpreting the Bible. Such skills include but are not limited to learning how to contextualise Scripture, to Bible-check (as opposed to merely fact-checking), to cross compare with other sources, and to evaluate the validity of arguments in commentaries, etc.

Oftentimes in Sunday services, the congregation listens to the preaching of the sermon, but seldom do they gain insights into the interpretive process of the preacher. What questions were asked? How was the interpretation arrived at? What contextual and intertextual references were made? How was the accuracy of the interpretation arrived at? What resources and tools were used and how?

Of course, not all these questions need to be addressed all the time but at times, showing how the preacher has reached an interpretation may provide models for the kinds of critical reading and thinking that lay persons can themselves apply in studying the Word. Local churches can also organise introductory classes in hermeneutics for their church members who want to be further equipped with the skills to study the Word as they lead others to do so in their discipleship groups. While there is a place for advanced hermeneutical studies in seminaries, church leaders also have a responsibility to develop foundational hermeneutical literacy in their congregation.

3. RIGHT ACTION IS CHARACTERISED BY JUSTICE AS RIGHTEOUSNESS AND LOVE

The oft-cited verse on justice is Micah 6:8: "He has told you, O man, what is good; and what does the Lord require of you but to do justice, and to love kindness, and to walk humbly with your God?" Here, we see that justice is tied to doing; it is realised in concrete action rather than in passivity.

What does justice as righteousness mean in concrete terms? With regards to our personal walk, it means pursuing holiness, not being conformed to the ways of the world but being continually transformed by the renewing of our minds (Rom. 12:2) so that we will be like Christ in our ways of thinking, feeling, and acting in the world.

With regards to our relations with others, it means acting in ways that are just towards others. Another concept commonly associated with justice in the Old Testament is the Hebrew word *meshar* which refers to equity as tied to fairness, evenness, and rightness. Equity is connected to God's righteous character (e.g., Ps. 98:9, "He will judge the world with righteousness, and the peoples with equity") but it is also concretised in the ways we treat the poor—Isaiah 11:3–4a,

> *And his delight shall be in the fear of the LORD.*
> *He shall not judge by what his eyes see,*
> *or decide disputes by what his ears hear,*
> *but with righteousness he shall judge the poor,*
> *and decide with equity for the meek of the earth;*

Equity is a more powerful concept than equality because while equality means treating everyone the same despite their background, equity recognises that each person may have different contexts, starting points, and access to resources and opportunities in life. An interesting metaphor is as follows: "Equality is giving everyone a shoe; equity is giving everyone a shoe that fits."[2]

When churches seek to pursue social justice, we should not understand the oppressed from our own lens or experiences. Rather, the Church should seek first to understand the context and concerns of the oppressed from their perspective and consider ways to empower them to overcome oppression. To treat the oppressed with equity entails a commitment to understanding them, and to probing deeper into the issues they face that cannot simply be resolved by easy claims to equal opportunity.

As discussed earlier, justice as righteousness also encompasses justice as love. Likewise, churches are to exemplify just communities and this is demonstrated in concrete ways through active engagements with oppressed groups; by demonstrating compassion, generosity in action, defending and speaking for them, and empowering them to be independent. Perhaps the challenge for the Church is finding the balance between righteousness and love in our acts of social justice. In some cases, the Church's work in social justice can itself become an aggressive push for righteousness with little evidence of love for people beyond those that she is defending. In other cases, the Church may emphasise acts of love through uplifting programmes with little thought about helping people turn to God's ways.

CONCLUSION

As political wokeism becomes even more pervasive along with its combinations of postmodernism and post-truth, new challenges will continue to arise. I hope that this book may provide a starting point for Christians to reflect on how to interpret the present time and respond accordingly. In this chapter, I have provided some practical suggestions and it is likely that churches are already working to support various social-global causes to different degrees, such as creation care, mental health counselling, social work to the needy, etc. Let me offer one more thought.

In today's hyperconnected digital age, the Church needs to also consider how to out-narrate "woke" culture on social media networks. One way is to model truth-seeking in our interpretations of events and practise justice as righteousness and love. Supposing a news item goes viral tomorrow, instead of jumping on the bandwagon by taking sides and being a "keyboard warrior", Christians can counter the barrage of negativity and one-sidedness by demonstrating empathy, discernment, and truth-seeking.

Supposing a trending issue pressures people to take sides in the name of racism, sexism, and other isms, Christians can counter divisions by demonstrating perspective-taking and being a bridge-builder across groups. When we respond to "woke" issues, Christians can rise above culture by demonstrating Christ-likeness and the fruit of the Spirit (Gal. 5:22–23)—love, joy, peace, patience, kindness, goodness, faithfulness, gentleness, and self-control.

As a Church, we must continually strive to find ways that Christian wokeness can tell the world a bigger story. One that replaces modern scepticism with certainty, self-centredness with supportive relationships, and resistance with love established on God's invitation to reconcile humanity to Himself.

〰️ REFLECTION QUESTIONS

1. Read Acts 2:42–47. In what ways did the early church demonstrate social justice? What empowered them to do so?

2. Before we attempt to enact social justice, how should we first pursue right interpretation? Pick a trending issue and show how you would apply critical literacy as well as biblical principles to interpreting this.

3. What are some ways your church can balance righteousness and love in practising acts of social justice? Provide concrete examples.

RESOURCES

A. On Christian Social Justice

1. Corbett, Steve & Brian Fikkert. *When Helping Hurts: How to Alleviate Poverty Without Hurting the Poor and Yourself*. Chicago, IL: Moody Publishers, 2014.

   The authors provide important principles and frameworks for the Church to effectively help the poor through understanding the complexities of poverty.

2. Keller, Timothy. *Generous Justice: How God's Grace Makes Us Just*. New York: Penguin, 2010.

   The author argues that justice for the poor and marginalised is central to scripture and biblical concepts of justice and grace can provide a basis for modern human rights.

3. Lim, Kar Yong. "'For All of You Are One in Christ Jesus' (Gal 3:28): Paul's Social Vision Beyond Inclusivity and Diversity." In *From Malaysia to the Ends of the Earth: Southeast Asian and Diasporic Contributions to Biblical and Theological Studies*, edited by Elaine Wei-Fun Goh, Kah-Jin Jeffrey Kuan, Jonathan Yun-Ka Tan, and Amos Wai-Ming Yong, 83–116. Claremont Press, 2021. http://www.jstor.org/stable/j.ctv2b07vst.8.

   The author provides an insightful understanding of Paul's social vision that tackles forms of ethnic and gender discrimination relevant for a biblical understanding of inclusivity and diversity.

4. Westfall, Cynthia Long & Bryan R. Dyer (Eds.). *The Bible and Social Justice: Old Testament and New Testament Foundations for the Church's Urgent Call*. Eugene, OR: Wipf and Stock Publishers, 2009.

This edited volume provides the perspectives of various biblical scholars on social justice in the Bible.

B. On Christian Perspectives to Political Wokeism, Postmodernism and Post-truth

5. Groothuis, Douglas. *Truth Decay: Defending Christianity Against the Challenges of Postmodernism*. Downers Grove, IL: InterVarsity Press, 2009.

   The author helps us understand the dangers of postmodernism and provides a solid defense of a Christian theology of truth.

6. Ott, Kate M. *Christian Ethics for a Digital Society*. Lanham, MD: Rowman & Littlefield, 2019.

   The author highlights important social shifts as a result of digital technology that is relevant to understanding post-truth and suggests how we can respond based on Christian values.

7. Strachan, Owen & John MacArthur. *Christianity and Wokeness: How the Social Justice Movement Is Hijacking the Gospel—and the Way to Stop It*. Washington, DC: Salem Books, 2021.

   The authors are critical of contemporary wokeism and argue why it is incompatible with Christianity.

8. Watkin, Christopher. *Biblical Critical Theory*. Grand Rapids, MI: Zondervan, 2022.

   The author goes beyond engaging with contemporary critical theory by offering a biblical theory that shows how the bible's unfolding narrative and key principles can help us better understand modern culture.

ENDNOTES

CHAPTER 1

1. Giattino, Charlie and Esteban Ortiz-Ospina. "Are We Working More Than Ever?" *In Our World in Data*, 2020, https://ourworldindata.org/working-more-than-ever.
2. Greene, Maxine. *Releasing the Imagination: Essays on Education, the Arts, and Social Change*. San Francisco, CA: Jossey-Bass, 1995.
3. Yeung, Jessie. "USC Professor Under Fire After Using Chinese Expression Students Allege Sounds Like English Slur". *CNN*, September 10, 2020. https://edition.cnn.com/2020/09/10/us/usc-chinese-professor-racism-intl-hnk-scli/index.html.
4. Bovon, Francis. *Luke 2: A Commentary on the Gospel of Luke 9:51–19:27*, translated by Donald S. Deer. Minneapolis, MN: Fortress Press, 2013.
5. Chen, Diane G. *Luke: A New Covenant Commentary*. Eugene, OR: Cascade Books, 2017; Parsons, Mikeal C. *Luke*. Grand Rapids, MI: Baker Academic, 2015.
6. Stott, John. *The Contemporary Christian*. Westmont, IL: InterVarsity Press, 1992, p. 28.
7. Anderson, Benedict. *Imagined Communities: Reflections on the Origin and Spread of Nationalism*. London, UK: Verso, 2006.
8. Niebuhr, Richard. *Christ and Culture*. New York: Harper & Row, 1951.
9. Watkin, Christopher. *Biblical Critical Theory*. Grand Rapids, MI: Zondervan, 2022, p. 21.

CHAPTER 2

1. United Nations Department of Economic and Social Affairs. *World Youth Report: Youth Civic Engagement*. New York: United Nations, 2016, p. 74.

2. National Youth Council. *The State of Youth in Singapore: Youth & Their Diverse Priorities*. Singapore: National Youth Council, 2021, pp. 13-14, 21.
3. Butler, Judith. *Gender Trouble: Feminism and the Subversion of Identity*. New York: Routledge, 1990.
4. Crenshaw, Kimberlé. "Demarginalizing the Intersection of Race and Sex: A Black Feminist Critique of Antidiscrimination Doctrine, Feminist Theory and Antiracist Politics." *University of Chicago Legal Forums* 1, no. 8 (1989): 139-167.
5. Lyotard, Jean-Francois. *The Postmodern Condition: A Report on Knowledge*, translated by Geoff Bennington and Brian Massumi. Minneapolis, MN: University of Minnesota Press, 1979, p. xxiv.
6. Sim, Stuart. "Postmodernism and Philosophy". In *The Routledge Companion to Postmodernism*, edited by Stuart Sim. New York: Routledge, 2011, pp. 3-14.
7. Lyotard, p. 9.
8. Baudrillard, Jean. "The Precession of Simulacra". In *The Norton Anthology of Theory and Criticism*, edited by Vincent B. Leitch, 1732-1741. New York: W.W. Norton, 1981.
9. Oxford Languages. "Word of the Year 2016". 2016, https://languages.oup.com/word-of-the-year/2016/.
10. Zygmunt Bauman. *Postmodern Ethics*. Malden, MA: Blackwell, 1993, p. 31.
11. Ott, Kate M. *Christian Ethics for a Digital Society*. Lanham, MD: Rowman & Littlefield, 2019, p. 66.
12. Ott, pp. 75-76.
13. Brady, William J., Killian McLoughlin, Tian N. Doan and Molly J. Crockett. "How Social Learning Amplifies Moral Outrage Expression in Online Social Networks". *Science Advances* 7 no. 33 (2021): 1-14. https://doi.org/10.1126/sciadv.abe5641.
14. Manshadi, Vahideh. "Study: An Abundance of Media Fuels Polarization". *Yale Insights*, March 9, 2022, https://insights.som.yale.edu/insights/study-an-abundance-of-media-fuels-polarization.
15. Sharma, Shweta. "Dalai Lama: The Significance of 'Tongue Greet-

ings' in Tibetan Culture". *Independent*, April 14, 2023. https://www.independent.co.uk/asia/india/dalai-lama-tongue-kissing-greeting-tibet-b2319738.html.

16. Butler, pp. 183–193.

CHAPTER 3

1. Behr, Thomas C. *Social Justice and Subsidiarity: Luigi Taparelli and the Origins of Modern Catholic Social Thought*. Washington, DC: Catholic University of America Press, 2019.

2. Burke, Tomas Patrick. "The Origins of Social Justice: Taparelli D'Azeglio". *Intercollegiate Studies Institute*, https://isi.org/intercollegiate-review/the-origins-of-social-justice-taparelli-dazeglio/.

3. Youngblood, Kevin J. *Jonah: God's Scandalous Mercy*, 2nd ed. Grand Rapids, MI: Zondervan, 2019, p. 51.

4. Brown, Francis, S. R. Driver, and Charles A. Briggs. *A Hebrew and English Lexicon of the Old Testament*. Boston, MA: Houghton Mifflin, 1907, pp. 877–878; Koehler, Ludwig, and Walter Baumgartner. *The Hebrew and Aramaic Lexicon of the Old Testament* Vol. 2. Leiden, Netherlands: Brill, 2001, pp. 1086–1087.

5. Sandel, Michael J. *Justice: What's the Right Thing To Do?* New York: Farrar, Straus, and Giroux, 2009.

6. Kant, Immanuel. *Foundations of the Metaphysics of Morals*, 2nd ed., translated by L. W. Beck. Upper Saddle River, NJ: Prentice-Hall, 1995 (Original work published 1785).

7. Youngblood, p. 57.

8. Sasson, Jack M. *Jonah, Anchor Bible Commentary*. New Haven, CT: Yale University Press, 1990, p. 69; Youngblood, p. 54.

9. Youngblood, p. 56.

10. Stuart, Douglas. *Hosea-Jonah, Word Biblical Commentary*. Nashville, TN: Thomas Nelson, 1987, p. 45.

11. Cooper, Alan. "In Praise of Divine Caprice: The Significance of the Book of Jonah". In *Among the Prophets: Language, Image and Structure in the Prophetic Writings*, edited by Philip R. Davies and

David J. A. Clines. London, UK: Bloomsbury, 2009, pp. 144–163; Tiemeyer, Lena-Sofia. "'Peace For Our Time': Reading Jonah in Dialogue with Abravanel in the Book of Twelve". *Journal of Hebrew Scriptures* 17 (2017). https://doi.org/10.5508/jhs.2017.v17.a6.

12. Wright, C. J. H. *Old Testament Ethics for the People of God*. Nottingham, UK: Inter-Varsity Press, 2004.
13. Brown, Francis, S. R. Driver, and Charles A. Briggs, p. 339; Clines, David J. A., ed. *Dictionary of Classical Hebrew Vol. 3*. Sheffield, UK: Sheffield Phoenix Press, 2010, p. 281; Koehler, Ludwig, and Walter Baumgartner, p. 337.
14. Gershom Scholem and Eric J. Schwab. "On Jonah and the Concept of Justice". *Critical Inquiry* 25, no. 2 (Winter 1999): 354.
15. Youngblood, p. 180.

CHAPTER 4

1. Groothuis, Douglas. *Truth Decay: Defending Christianity Against the Challenges of Postmodernism*. Downers Grove, IL: InterVarsity Press, 2009.
2. Minow, Martha. "Equality vs. Equity". *American Journal of Law and Equality* 1 (2021): 167–193.

ABOUT THE AUTHOR

Dr Suzanne Choo is an Associate Professor at the National Institute of Education, Nanyang Technological University. She taught at a Christian mission secondary school in Singapore for six years before pursuing her Master of Arts in English Studies at the National University of Singapore and her PhD in English Education at Columbia University in the United States.

During her time in the United States, she served as a volunteer to a Christian non-profit organisation that runs a soup kitchen via a mobile bus to impoverished communities. This experience was one of several that moved her to pursue theological studies and uncover its connections to social justice.

She holds a Graduate Diploma in Christian Studies and the Interdisciplinary Studies Prize from the Biblical Graduate School of Theology (BGST) in Singapore where she is currently pursuing her Master of Arts in Theology and Integrative Studies. She worships at Adam Road Presbyterian Church together with her husband, Wilson, and their daughter. Her website is http://suzannechoo.com.

Churches are called to "make disciples of all the nations" in a faithful and relevant manner through both word and deed. This is no easy task given our ever-evolving world where a multitude of complex social issues confront the Church.

The Gospel Way series provides practical handles to help Christians address such issues. The series has seven distinctives. It is:

1. Christ-centred, emphasising how the gospel speaks into each social issue.

2. Contextualised, written by Asians for Asians.

3. Curated, taking trustworthy positions on theological matters.

4. Church-focused, written pastorally for use in church.

5. Concise, designed with busy people in mind.

6. Convenient, written in a reader-friendly style.

7. Concrete, helping the reader to apply practical insights to their lives.

GRACEW♥RKS

Graceworks is a publishing and training consultancy based in Singapore dedicated to promoting relational transformation in church and society, and seeing lives transformed through books that present truth for life.

Our publications can be found on
www.graceworks.com.sg/store
and at major online book retailers.

Get in touch with us at *enquiries@graceworks.com.sg*
or follow us @GraceworksSG.

www.ingramcontent.com/pod-product-compliance
Lightning Source LLC
LaVergne TN
LVHW010408070526
838199LV00065B/5917